HACKED

ז
פריצה
ה
ו
ת

RESTORING
STOLEN IDENTITY
AND EMBRACING THE
INHERITED BLESSING

THE HEBREW
CHRISTIAN

HACKED! THE HEBREW CHRISTIAN

Restoring Stolen Identity and Embracing the Inherited Blessing

BY:

KENNETH S. ALBIN

For more information about Kenneth S. Albin

www.savethenations.com

Special thanks for artwork, pictures & cover design:
Mike and Carolina Hernandez
Mike@tnstudionsinc.com

TABLE OF CONTENTS

DESCRIPTIONS

WHAT ARE THE MOEDIM?

The Moedim are appointed days, rehearsals and special set times that God invites His people to gather as a congregation to meet with Him, their Creator and King. In God's sovereignty He has chosen, from the beginning of creation, seven appointed times during His calendar year.

WHAT IS THE SABBATH?

God has also, in His sovereignty, chosen another day that is set apart from the rest. God has pre-determined, by His sovereignty, to set apart the seventh day as the Sabbath for man to rest and to honor the Creator. The Sabbath was created for all of mankind, not just the Jew, Israel, but for all mankind.

WHAT IS A CHRISTIAN?

The word Christian is mentioned three times in the New Testament. It is the Greek word *Christianos*. The term means "to be a little Christ" or "anointed". The term is used to point to a true disciple of Jesus Christ. A Christian is committed to following Jesus Christ, His teachings, His ways and His commands. The disciple of Christ will become more and more like Jesus as the Holy Spirit continues to work and conform their lives to the will of God. A real Christian has been born again and passed from death to life and darkness to the kingdom of Light. (Acts 11:26, Acts 26:28, 1 Peter 4:16, John 5:24, Colossians 1:13,)

WHO ARE THE JEWS?

The word Jew is a term used to describe those from the Southern Kingdom, tribe of Judah or the house of Judah. A Jew may also be from the tribe of Benjamin since that was the tribe given to David's descendants by the prophet Ahijah when he divided the two kingdoms and gave ten tribes to Jeroboam and two tribes to Solomon's son, Rehoboam. In the Southern Kingdom of Judah there were also some from the tribe of Levi and remnants of other tribes. Later these from the Southern House of Israel would also be known as being Jews or Jewish. The title Jew was first used in the bible just before, during and then following the captivity in Babylon. You can see this in the book of Esther and the books of Ezra and Nehemiah. The Northern Kingdom with ten tribes became commonly known as the house of Israel.

WHAT IS A GENTILE?

The term *Gentile* comes from the Hebrew word *Goy* or its plural *Goyim.* It refers to the nations who were not physical descendants of Israel. A Gentile can also be used of the house of Israel, sometimes known as Ephraim, who lost their inheritance and identity when they, in their apostasy and divorce from Yahweh, were scattered to the nations, never to return. They are commonly referred to as the lost tribes of Israel. When a person accepts Jesus, he is "grafted-in" to Israel and becomes connected to and a descendant of Abraham by faith. It is important to understand that a Christian and follower of Jesus is no longer a Gentile. (2 Kings 17:23, Ephesians 2:11-19)

WHAT IS A HEBREW?

A *Hebrew* is the term meaning “one from beyond” or “crossed over one”. It refers to Abram who crossed over the Euphrates River into a land that was promised by the God who revealed Himself as the true and living God. Abram crossed over spiritually to forsake his father’s idols and worship El Shaddai.

WHAT IS A HEBREW CHRISTIAN?

Though the term Hebrew is not common or usually connected to Christians, but it should be. A Christian is a person who has crossed over from death to life and from darkness to light. This person is a disciple of Jesus Christ and follows His teachings. The term Messiah or Messianic is actually synonymous to the word Christian. Both words come are derived from anointed one from what the Jews call Mashiach or Messiah.

A Hebrew Christian is a person who also embraces their inheritance and identity in connection to Abraham. The Hebrew Christian understands that they are not separated from, but supernaturally connected to Israel through the blood of Jesus & His death, burial and resurrection. The Hebrew Christian receives by faith the benefits of that rich tree and identity. A Hebrew Christian because of grace and truth receives a new identity and inheritance and now gets to walk in the light of the Torah by the power of the Holy Spirit.

In no way is a Christian or a Hebrew Christian ever to think they replace natural Israel or the Jewish people. This is a dangerous and demonic doctrine that has caused many to horrors in the past. The Hebrew Christian is no longer hacked and no longer has their identity and inheritance stolen. They begin to see the Shalom of God working mightily "Nothing Missing, Nothing Broken, Nothing Lost, All Restored!"

WHAT IS TORAH?

Most commonly this refers to the first five books of the Bible known as the Pentateuch. The Torah can also refer to the entire Old Testament known as the Tanakh. Many think it means "law" or a book of "do's and don'ts", but this incorrect. The truest understanding of Torah is "instruction and teaching". The root word for Torah is *yarah* and it is an archery term meaning, "to hit the mark".

Throughout the Scriptures the promise of good things, life and well-being is connected and given to those who obey Torah. The New & Old Testament word for *sin* means "to miss the mark". So when we obey Torah we "hit the mark" and live well, but when we sin by disobeying the Torah we get the consequences. The Torah, God's Voice and God's Word are all synonymous. (Deuteronomy 4:40, 5:29, Proverbs 6:23, Psalm 119:105)

INTRODUCTION

We've been Hacked! The term "Hacked" has been now been widely used to explain the violation and horror of identity theft. In the digital age, which we live, it is a common occurrence where we feel we have almost no defense. If you have been hacked, your life is disrupted by the theft of your identity including vital and very personal information. It can affect almost everything in your life. You can spend a great deal of time and money within the legal system to right this wrong, but many times the horror can go on for years.

That identity theft can hurt your name and credit and can muddle even your history. Being hacked is being stolen from and hits you at your core because your life revolves around your true identity. Spiritually speaking, Jesus told us that there was a thief who wanted to steal, kill and destroy. It is interesting that Jesus taught this during Hanukkah, the Festival of Lights. Satan, like an angel of light through confusion, deception and misinterpretation has stolen the true identity of Christians. In John chapter 10 Jesus speaks about another fold of sheep that will be restored to the One True Shepherd. Perhaps He was inferring to the ones whose identity had been hacked as well and were now lost without hope, and a Shepherd Who would lead them back.

As I sit to begin writing this book I am feeling compelled to answer, with grace and truth, the many questions and confusion revolving the identity of believers in Christ whether they are born Jewish, Gentile or perhaps even what is known as the lost tribes of Israel. Before I begin, I want to preface my thoughts to come from, first of all the Holy Scriptures contained in the Old and New Testaments, and secondly any historical and cultural references, which are relevant to our subject. I am aware of the many different and varied opinions that have been expressed and are currently easily available on the web and media. I will be endeavoring to expose and explain what is known as a Hebrew Christian and how this term came to be. Please know that many traditional teachings and traditions of the Christian Faith have swayed from the original intentions because of the departure from the Hebraic roots of the faith. I am using the term Hebraic instead of Jewish because the term Jewish or Judaism comes from the son of Israel named Judah in which King David was a descendant. The term of Judah in the day, which we live, in most people's minds, is the same as all the tribes and children of Israel. I will explain in this book the misnomer and misunderstanding of that thinking. It has been widely propagated and endorsed, but once it is exposed it will make way for one of the greatest mysteries and love stories you will ever know.

For those who don't know me, I was born in New York and moved to Florida like so many fleeing the cold when I was just eleven. My parents made sure I went to Hebrew school and I had my Bar Mitzvah at Temple Beth Israel as a good Jewish boy at thirteen. At that time I was unaware my life would take such a different turn when my "born again" dad took me to his new church, which happened to have the grandfather of now my wife leading it.

When I saw the changed man my father was it made me aware of a real higher Power and plan for my life. I believe Destiny has a way of finding you! It found me at fifteen years old and I have never looked back as Yeshua Messiah became my Lord and made me the blessed man I am today.

In those early days I felt somehow I needed to forget my Hebrew roots as I became a pastor. My wife made me go to Israel, which I had no desire to do, but from that plane ride over, something got reignited in me. Slowly but surely I began embracing and teaching the Bible with a different perspective than many of my colleagues. I would see things with different eyes and a different mindset when I read the Bible. It was so different than what I had been taught in Church about God.

The Hebrew mindset is one that is founded in God's love for Israel. God chose the smallest and least people and set His love on them. So for now, over thirty years I have been pastoring in some capacity, and truthfully and humbly I don't think I had a clue until a short time ago. It has taken me so long to realize what Jesus meant when He said to "Go and make disciples of all Nations, teaching them to observe all I commanded you."

So, you might have picked up this book and saw the title "HACKED! The Hebrew Christian" and are thinking "They don't go together. You are either a Hebrew or a Christian, but you can't be both…" Or can you? I promise as you read this book you will see what I mean by this and yes, yes, & yes! Not only can you be a Hebrew Christian, but hopefully you will come to embrace that as your true identity before we are done.

Finally, please don't read this with the assumption that what you read will be bringing you into another system of control or legalism like in the movie "The Matrix"! I promise what you read will do the very opposite, it will free you as one who knows the Truth and will forever live in the revelation of that identity now restored. Well, enough said, now let's begin.

Chapter One:

"What is a Hebrew?"

Who are you? It is the quest of every life. If you have grown up in church you would have been taught about your identity as a believer from a "Before I accepted Christ" (B.C.) or "After I accepted Christ." (The "Ken B.C." was a mess!)

A common teaching is that when you accept and believe in Christ according to 2 Corinthians 5:17: "Therefore, if anyone is in Christ, he is a new creation; old things have passed away; behold, all things have become new."

We also know that Christ is the English term for the Hebrew word Messiah meaning "Anointed One" or "His Anointed." There is a truth about identity found in the scriptures, for much of our identity comes from our bloodline or DNA. Many people don't like to read the genealogies listed in the Bible and think of them as boring or irrelevant for today. But hidden in these bloodlines are the secrets and mysteries of the identity and places of what we read about in the Bible. Your natural identity and bloodline comes from your relatives and has implications that affect your biology, psychology, personality and so much more!

My wife and I at the time of this writing are enjoying our two-year-old granddaughter, Brielle, and I can tell you from observation she came from the womb with her ancestors' attributes in her. She has these traits in her bloodline and it is a part of her identity and who she will become no matter how hard she might not want to be like any of them when they are realized.

So, if you are a believer in Christ, then it means that His bloodline and family tree are a part of you, too! I need to show you this in the Bible. It means you came from something and have been given, by God's sovereignty and grace, a family heritage which gives you a right to an inheritance and blessing you might not even know exists.

To begin to understand your identity it is important to glean and look backwards in time and see the spiritual father of all those who live by faith. It would be oh, so wonderful if everything in life could be simple with no complications, but if you are like me you know real life is seldom without some kind of disorder. Well, the man known as the "Father of us all" who lived by faith is no exception to the muddles and missteps we have all made. Even though Abram, as he is first known, makes some huge blunders, he also did some amazing things that are examples to anyone who desires to understand and live in their true identity and faith. You see, if you read the Bible with the correct set of lenses you will find out that

Abram was not even "Jewish." In fact, Abram came from a place called the "Ur of the Chaldees."

Abram believed the Lord, and he credited it to him as righteousness. 7 He also said to him, "I am the Lord, who brought you out of Ur of the Chaldeans to give you this land to take possession of it." Genesis 15:6-7 NIV

The land of Ur was a city of Mesopotamia that bordered the western side of the Euphrates River. Abram had been with his father, Terah, his wife, Sarai and his nephew, Lot in Harran before Abram had a life-changing encounter and entered by faith into a covenant agreement with the True and Living God. What many people don't know is that Abram had a father who was an idol maker and captain in the evil King Nimrod's kingdom. Abram, when he was in his fifties, destroyed his father's idols because he realized an idol could not create, give or sustain life. It wasn't until Abram was seventy-five years old that the call of God came to him to leave his father, his family and his culture to completely follow Yahweh, the Living God by faith and obedience through revelation.

Now, being what is called "Jewish" was not even on the radar yet. A Jew is one who is actually a descendant of Jacob or his God-given changed name of Israel. A Jew is not just a descendent of Israel, but specifically of one of his sons named Judah. This is where the term Jewish comes from. Abram is never called nor was a Jew, but he is known by a different term that is very important for anyone who claims Abraham as his or her spiritual father of faith.

Then one who had escaped came and told Abram the Hebrew, for he dwelt by the terebinth trees of Mamre the Amorite, brother of Eshcol and brother of Aner; and they were allies with Abram. Genesis 14:13

The first time we see the word Hebrew in the Bible it is found in this scripture that talks about Abram. It will for sure not be the last time, for in the same book of Genesis a "great-grandson" of Abraham will be identified as a Hebrew as well. His name is Joseph and he has been sent by the providence of God to preserve the posterity of his family's legacy and mission.

So what does being Hebrew really mean? In the Strong's Concordance it says it is "one from beyond." The root of the word in Hebrew gives a more telling clue of its meaning. The root word eber or heber means "to come from the region across the stream or river" and could also mean to "pass over" or "pass through."

In biblical times it meant that Abram and his descendants had crossed over from the other side, specifically the Euphrates River. It was God who told Abram to leave and settle in the land of Canaan and a promise was given to Abram and his descendants to possess the land as an inheritance of God. The very name "Hebrew" has a connotation of temporary or a sojourning people. If we follow this theme through the New Testament book of Hebrews, look what we read about Abraham.

By faith Abraham obeyed when he was called to go out to the place which he would receive as an inheritance. And he went out, not knowing where he was going. 9 By faith he dwelt in the land of promise as in a foreign country, dwelling in tents with Isaac and Jacob, the heirs with him of the same promise; 10 for he waited for the city which has foundations, whose builder and maker is God. 13 These all died in faith, not having received the promises, but having seen them afar off were assured of them, embraced them and confessed that they were strangers and pilgrims on the earth. 14 For those who say such things declare plainly that they seek a homeland. 15 And truly if they had called to mind that country from which they had come out, they would have had opportunity to return. 16 But now they desire a better, that is, a heavenly country. Therefore God is not ashamed to be called their God, for He has prepared a city for them. Hebrews 11:8-10, 13-16 NKJV

Abraham is known as a Hebrew because he crossed, over not just a physical barrier, but also a spiritual barrier to leave his family, his father and all the ways of the world, to worship and follow Yahweh God. In fact, the seal or mark of circumcision in the body was a physical sign of the covenant that pointed to the fact that the spiritual barrier would one day be completely removed through Christ.

The Bible says that Abraham went out by faith, not knowing where he was going. This is the walk of faith we are to follow as believers, as Christians following Jesus. Let's look at some powerful scriptures that identify us with

Abraham as our spiritual father. This is important because your identity is forever tied to Abraham through Jesus.

Chapter One:

PERSONAL OR SMALL GROUP STUDY

1. Abram was not even __________. In fact Abram came from a place called the Ur of the Chaldees.

2. A ______is one who is actually a descendant of Jacob or his God given changed name of ___________.

3. So, what does being ______________ really mean? In the Strong's concordance it says it is "one from __________."

4. Abraham is known as a Hebrew because he _______ over not just a physical barrier, but also a ______________ barrier to leave his family, his father and all the ways of the world to ___________ and follow Yahweh God.

5. In your own words describe what you thought the word Hebrew meant before you read this chapter and also what you realize it means now.

____

____

____

____

____

6. The Bible says that Abraham went out by __________ not knowing where he was going.

7. What does it mean to you to live by faith?

____

____

____

____

____

8. The mark or seal of circumcision in the body will point to what?

____

____

____

____

____

Chapter Two:

"Your Father, Abraham"

If you belong to Christ, then you are Abraham's seed, and heirs according to the promise. Galatians 3:29 NIV

One of the most powerful promises and revelations in the Bible is the scripture you just read! Many Christians have not been taught the roots of their faith nor their true identity. You might have heard or gathered from your own mind that if you believe in Jesus you are a now a new creation and as a believer you are in the new covenant and that everything else has now been deemed unnecessary because of Christ. But what if our true identity has been hacked? What would you do if you just found out you were connected to a wealthy family member who has left you an inheritance in another country and heritage you didn't know you were connected to, and the inheritance was just waiting for you? You just found out you were a legal heir and it was yours! If that happened nothing would stop you from claiming your legal rights.

The Galatian people were mostly those not born into Judaism and were coming from the pagan nations who did not worship the God of Israel. Look what Paul the Apostle tells these who were not familiar with Abraham and the covenant God had made with him.

He then tells them that when they are truly belonging to Christ (Messiah-Anointed One) that they have now become the seed, or descendant of Abraham. He also tells them they are now the legal heirs of the inheritance and promises that were given to Abraham and his descendants. This is one of the greatest mysteries and has been hidden from most Christians. The fact is that Christ has given you a spiritual blood transfusion and you now have the DNA of a descendant of Abraham. That means if it was promised to Abraham and his seed, it is promised to you regardless of your native born bloodline. This also means that you can trace your family tree back to Abraham. In your family tree you not only have Judah, but all the tribes of Israel. From Abraham came Isaac, then Jacob (Israel) and all his sons, both natural and adopted. You came from the seed of Abraham! If you believe in Jesus you can trace your physical family tree as Abraham's descendant. Most Christians don't ever fully realize this, but now it's up to you to embrace your roots, family lineage and the inheritance it gives you as a person who can trace his identity back to the one who crossed over into true worship, your father, Abraham.

I want you to say right now, "I am a Hebrew, I am an Israelite, I am of the seed of Abraham." Now, you don't have to say it or even believe it, but I'd like for you to do so, by faith, and believe it for this reason…not because you have to, but because you get to! This is what I teach the people in my church and to people when I travel, when it comes to all the promises and instructions God has given us. We, as those who are grafted in to Israel, get to enjoy all the blessings and the richness of our heritage.

Are they Hebrews? So am I. Are they Israelites? So am I. Are they descendants of Abraham? So am I. 2 Corinthians 11:22 NLT

The richness of your inheritance is through Christ and what He did to establish a restoration and a new identity.

Understand, then, that those who have faith are children of Abraham. 8 Scripture foresaw that God would justify the Gentiles by faith, and announced the gospel in advance to Abraham: "All nations will be blessed through you." 9 So those who rely on faith are blessed along with Abraham, the man of faith.
Galatians 3:7-9NIV

The Gospel that God preached to Abraham was that through his seed all the families of the earth would be grafted and intertwined into his family. The word for blessed in the Hebrew has the deeper understanding of being intertwined or grafted. This is what I discovered with some research about the Hebrew word for bless found in God's promise to Abraham.

[1] In five places in the Talmud and other Rabbinic literature, nivrecu is translated as "grafted or intermingled." In the Orthodox Jewish ArtScroll Tenakh Series, Volume 1, page 432, it is written: There is ... an opinion shared by Rashbam [to Genesis 28:14], Chizkuni, Da'as Zekeinum, and quoted by Tur that the verb (ve nivrecu) in Genesis 12:3 is related to the root barak as in the Mishnaic term mavreek meaning to "intermingle or graft." [cf Kelaim 7:1, Sotah 43a.] As Heidenheim explains it, this interpretation is inspired by the fact that nowhere else besides here do we find barak in the sense of blessing in the niphal conjugation, while in the sense of "grafting" it is common in that form. Therefore, based upon this insight of the Hebrew language by respected Hebrew scholars within the house of Judah (Judaism), Genesis (Bereishit) 12:3 is better understood to be translated as: "And in thee shall all families of the earth nivrecu [be grafted or intermingled]."

The reason this is so powerful is that now we can get a better understanding of where the Apostle Paul got the foundation and understanding of how the believing Gentiles are now grafted-in to the stock and root of Israel through Christ. It is explained in detail in Romans chapter 11.

Because Paul was a scholar of the Torah, he knew about the "grafting-in" to the one family and tree of Abraham from his Torah study. If we are to truly understand our identity then

---

1 http://www.waytozion.org/articles/restoretwohouse/12.Ephraim%20and%20Judah%20Become%20One%20House.pdf

we must not think it is permissible to somehow separate us from our roots, as our identity comes from our connection through the bloodline of Abraham. Remember, Abraham had to cross over and we must do the same, but in the case of identity we must now reconnect to our spiritual roots and embrace them.

The Rabbi's teach that Abraham, when he crossed over, was on the moral and spiritual side and the world was on the other. This "crossing over" was a type of being born again, a spiritual awakening, as Abram crossed over from the dark world of idolatry into the true worship that God was looking for "in spirit and in truth." This again is what has happens to every believer in Jesus. We cross over from the domain of darkness into the kingdom of Light. We are awakened out of our sleep as the Light of Christ shines on us. Hallelujah, for we are following in the faith of our father, Abraham.

Let's take another look at Romans chapter 11 and see if we can confirm our findings.

I say then, has God cast away His people? Certainly not! For I also am an Israelite, of the seed of Abraham, of the tribe of Benjamin. 2 God has not cast away His people whom He foreknew.
Romans 11:1-2A NKJV

We can see from the beginning of the chapter Paul identifies himself as an Israelite of the seed of Abraham, and specifically of the tribe of Benjamin, who was the one tribe given to Judah and David when the kingdoms of Judah and

Israel were torn and divided after the death of Solomon due to all his idolatry and wicked behavior. We can see that Paul is identifying with, and not separating, his new identity in Christ from Israel and Abraham. He is actually solidifying and confirming it!

I say then, have they stumbled that they should fall? Certainly not! But through their fall, to provoke them to jealousy, salvation has come to the Gentiles. 12 Now if their fall is riches for the world, and their failure riches for the Gentiles, how much more their fullness! 13 For I speak to you Gentiles; inasmuch as I am an apostle to the Gentiles, I magnify my ministry, 14 if by any means I may provoke to jealousy those who are my flesh and save some of them. 15 For if their being cast away is the reconciling of the world, what will their acceptance be but life from the dead? 16 For if the firstfruit is holy, the lump is also holy; and if the root is holy, so are the branches. 17 And if some of the branches were broken off, and you, being a wild olive tree, were grafted in among them, and with them became a partaker of the root and fatness of the olive tree, 18 do not boast against the branches. But if you do boast, remember that you do not support the root, but the root supports you. 19 You will say then, “Branches were broken off that I might be grafted in.” 20 Well said. Because of unbelief they were broken off, and you stand by faith. Do not be haughty, but fear. 21 For if God did not spare the natural branches, He may not spare you either. 22 Therefore consider the goodness and severity of God: on those who fell, severity; but toward you, goodness, if you continue in His goodness. Otherwise you also will be cut off. 23 And they also, if they do not continue in unbelief, will be grafted in, for God is able

to graft them in again. 24 For if you were cut out of the olive tree which is wild by nature, and were grafted contrary to nature into a cultivated olive tree, how much more will these, who are natural branches, be grafted into their own olive tree? 25 For I do not desire, brethren, that you should be ignorant of this mystery, lest you should be wise in your own opinion, that blindness in part has happened to Israel until the fullness of the Gentiles has come in. 26 And so all Israel will be saved, as it is written: "The Deliverer will come out of Zion, And He will turn away ungodliness from Jacob; 27 For this is My covenant with them, When I take away their sins.
" Romans 11:11-27 NKJV

The Apostle Paul could not have been clearer in this teaching. He explains how Israel, because of their sin, was severed like branches that have been broken off from their heritage and tree that represented their inheritance, blessing and prosperity. He uses the word "fullness" two times in this scripture. Once to point to the truth that in Israel's rejection the Gentiles have been made rich by being grafted-in. Second, to describe that when Israel is fully restored back to their God by accepting Messiah Jesus, it will be life from the dead. All twelve tribes of Israel will come back to God and the reunion will be a revival like no one has ever seen!

The second time the Apostle Paul uses the word "fullness" is when he teaches that Israel is now in blindness to their Messiah until the fullness of the Gentiles has come in. Did you know that the word for "Gentiles" is also "nations" or "Goyim?" God's love for Israel & Abraham was not to exclude the nations, but to be a Light to include every nation in the covenant blessing through Messiah. This is why in the previous chapter of Romans we hear this powerful declaration:

But what does it say? "The word is near you, in your mouth and in your heart" (that is, the word of faith which we preach): 9 that if you confess with your mouth the Lord Jesus and believe in your heart that God has raised Him from the dead, you will be saved. 10 For with the heart one believes unto righteousness, and with the mouth confession is made unto salvation. 11 For the Scripture says, "Whoever believes on Him will not be put to shame. 12 For there is no distinction between Jew and Greek, for the same Lord over all is rich to all who call upon Him. 13 For "whoever calls on the name of the Lord shall be saved." Romans 10:8-13 NKJV

The grafting in to the richness of the olive tree will continue until the fullness of the Gentiles comes in. Where did Paul get these thoughts and teachings? In Romans chapter 10 the Apostle quotes Deuteronomy chapter 30, Joel chapter 2 and Isaiah chapter 28. Surely a revelation like this has to have some type of witness in the Holy Scriptures? Thankfully, it does, and in what we are about to discover is a key to your identity and the right you can claim to all your inheritance.

Chapter Two:

PERSONAL OR GROUP STUDY

1. If you belong to Christ, then you are Abraham's _______, and __________ according to the promise. Galatians 3:29 NIV

2. What does it mean to you to be an heir?

____

____

____

____

3. The fact is that Christ has given you a spiritual blood _________________ and you now have the ________ of a descendant of Abraham.

4. If you believe in Jesus you can trace your physical family tree as _________________descendant.

5. "I am a ______________, I am an ______________, I am of the seed of ________________."

6. We as those who are _____________ in to Israel get to enjoy all the blessings and the richness of our

_____________.

7. The word for blessed in the Hebrew has the deeper understanding of being _______________ or ___________.

8. Abraham had to cross over and we must do the same, but in the case of _____________we must now reconnect to our spiritual ___________ and embrace them. How can you do that? ____

9. For I do not desire, brethren, that you should be ignorant of this mystery, lest you should be wise in your own opinion, that blindness in part has happened to Israel until the _____________of the __________ has come in. Romans 11:25

10. The crossing over was a type of being

__________________.

Chapter Three:

"The Adoption"

As we continue to look at Romans chapter 11, I want you to know what the process of grafting is. When I was a teenager, and when I was in my early years of marriage, my dad and I had a landscape business. It was there that I learned about grafting from a nursery I visited. I would see how they would take the trunk of a healthy and disease-resistant tree and attach a stem or a branch from another type of tree to the larger, stronger and healthy one. The upper portion is inserted into what is called the rootstock. Then the two trees will continue to grow as one united tree, which is what Paul is referring to in the book of Romans.

The process of grafting has been done for thousands of years. In a sense it connects a foreigner or stranger to something that has a strong root and established foundation. Now, isn't this what the Bible teaches about those nations and foreigners who did not have a covenant, revelation or access to Yahweh, the living God, but now get the same because they are now connected to the root and foundation of Abraham through Christ? I hope you are getting this and receiving it, for it is the true Gospel.

So now, let's look at where the term "fullness" of the nations or Gentiles actually comes from in the Bible. Do you remember the story of Joseph? It is a powerful story of the providence of God to fulfill what God told Abraham about those who would come from his loins. God told Abram before his name was changed that his people would be strangers and slaves in a land for four hundred years, but afterward they would come out with deliverance and great wealth and possessions. So how would this happen?

After the miracle child, Isaac there came his two sons, Jacob (Israel) and Esau. Jacob would eventually have twelve sons who will be known as the twelve tribes of Israel. However, during the process the brothers get jealous of the eldest son of Rachel, the wife that Jacob really loved. They conspired a plan to kill him, being tired of hearing of his dreams of greatness, but Judah steps in and convinces them to sell him for a profit to the Ishmaelite's from Midian. They happened to be on their way to Egypt where Joseph would go from the dry and waterless pit to the favor and temptation found in Potiphar's house, to the prison where Joseph will persevere with patience as he sees the power of dreams, and finally to find fulfillment in the palace, ruling with Pharaoh over Egypt.

It is here in Egypt that Joseph has two sons, Manasseh the first-born, and Ephraim the younger. Joseph tries to forget his past life and the hardships that brought him to this place.

Joseph was free, but in a prison of memories that haunted him.

As he longed for his family his brothers arrived requesting to buy the grain of Egypt. Joseph uses this to eventually get his younger blood sibling, Benjamin to come to Egypt. As Joseph reveals himself and asks them to all to come near, he is a prophetic picture of how God wants all to draw near to Messiah and find the One who will preserve their life and provide for them.

Joseph sends for his father, Israel with wagons of provision from Egypt. Israel had believed his son was dead, but a type of resurrection has occurred. The son that was dead was now not just alive, but bringing life to all the twelve sons and tribes of Israel. What a prophetic picture!

After Jacob (Israel) arrives he blesses Pharaoh and finds a new home in Goshen with his family. When he is old and ready to die, he asks to see Joseph and his grandsons, Manasseh and Ephraim. This is where the story takes a dramatic turn and has a great deal to do with the grafting in we have been talking about.

Now remember, these two sons of Joseph were born in Egypt. They had a pagan priest as a father-in-law and their mother was not of the family of Abraham or any of his descendants. Israel makes a bold statement to his son Joseph that most just skim over in the Bible, but it is very important.

Now it came to pass after these things that Joseph was told,
"Indeed your father is sick"; and he took with him his two
sons, Manasseh and Ephraim. 2 And Jacob was told, "Look,
your son Joseph is coming to you"; and Israel strengthened
himself and sat up on the bed. 3 Then Jacob said to Joseph:
"God Almighty appeared to me at Luz in the land of Canaan
and blessed me, 4 and said to me, 'Behold, I will make you
fruitful and multiply you, and I will make of you a multitude
of people, and give this land to your descendants after you as
an everlasting possession.' 5 And now your two sons,
Ephraim and Manasseh, who were born to you in the land of
Egypt before I came to you in Egypt, are mine; as Reuben and
Simeon, they shall be mine. 6 Your offspring whom you beget
after them shall be yours; they will be called by the name of
their brothers in their inheritance.
Genesis 48:1-6 NKJV

When Jacob sees Joseph he begins to repeat to Joseph what God had previously told to all the patriarchs beginning with Abraham. Immediately afterwards, he as a patriarch himself, declares without Joseph's foreknowledge or permission, that the two sons born in Egypt were now adopted into Israel just as much as Rueben and Simeon. Did you know that Reuben and Simeon were the first and second born to Israel respectively? So now what do you think this means? It means that Joseph's two sons are being adopted and given status and inheritance of the first and second born to Israel.

Now, Israel adopts the two sons of Egypt and "grafts them" if you will, into him. He also tells Joseph, "Even your other sons will be known by their name, not yours." This is why many times you will not see Joseph listed directly as a tribe, but rather you will see Manasseh and Ephraim in his place. Are you beginning to see the picture of the adoption that takes place in and through our heavenly Joseph?

But wait, it gets even better because Israel is about to bless his sons with a blessing. Remember according to Jacob (Israel) these two sons are now his sons by adoption and no longer belong to Joseph.

And Israel beheld Joseph's sons, and said, who are these? 9
And Joseph said to his father, they are my sons, whom God
has given me here. And he said, bring them, I pray thee, to
me, that I may bless them.10 But the eyes of Israel were
heavy from age: he could not see. And he brought them nearer
to him; and he kissed them, and embraced them.11 And Israel
said to Joseph, I had not thought to see thy face; and behold,
God has let me see also thy seed. 12 And Joseph brought them
out from his knees, and bowed down with his face to the
earth.13 And Joseph took them both, Ephraim in his right
hand toward Israel's left hand, and Manasseh in his left hand
toward Israel's right hand, and brought [them] near to him.14
But Israel stretched out his right hand, and laid [it] on
Ephraim's head—now he was the younger—and his left hand
on Manasseh's head; guiding his hands intelligently, for
Manasseh was the firstborn.15 And he blessed Joseph, and
said, The God before whom my fathers Abraham and Isaac
walked, the God that shepherded me all my life long to this
day,16 the Angel that redeemed me from all evil, bless the
lads; and let my name be named upon them, and the name of
my fathers Abraham and Isaac; and let them grow into a

multitude in the midst of the land!17 When Joseph saw that his father laid his right hand on the head of Ephraim, it was evil in his eyes; and he took hold of his father's hand to remove it from Ephraim's head to Manasseh's head.18 And Joseph said to his father, Not so, my father, for this is the firstborn: put thy right hand on his head.19 But his father refused and said, I know, my son, I know: he also will become a people, and he also will be great; but truly his younger brother will be greater than he; and his seed will become the fullness of nations.20 And he blessed them that day, saying, In thee will Israel bless, saying, God make thee as Ephraim and Manasseh! And he set Ephraim before Manasseh.21 And Israel said to Joseph, Behold, I die; and God will be with you, and bring you again to the land of your fathers.22 And *I* have given to thee one tract [of land] above thy brethren, which I took out of the hand of the Amorite with my sword and with my bow. Genesis 48:15-23 Darby

There are a lot of things happening here. Let me give you the bullet points, and then we can dive together into the deep truths found in this true and telling story.

- God allowed Jacob (Israel) to physically see the children of the son he believed was dead.

- Joseph brought Manasseh and Ephraim to Israel to receive a blessing from not just their grandfather a patriarch, but now the one who has adopted them and given them his name Israel.
- Israel blessed Joseph by recounting the blessing of the One who is his constant Shepherd and the One who sent His angel to redeem from him from all evil.

- Israel blessed the two sons by giving them his name, and blessed them to grow into a multitude in the land.

- Joseph was displeased because Israel had crossed his hands, putting his right hand and the double blessing upon Ephraim, the younger, and his left on Manasseh, the oldest.

- Israel blessed Ephraim saying that his seed would become the fullness of the nations.

- Israel then gives Joseph an additional portion above his brothers, which Jacob had taken from the Amorites with his sword and bow.

One of the physical and prophetic things that Israel did was to cross his hands and give the greater blessing to Ephraim, who was not born first and by the natural birth order, was not the rightful heir of the double portion blessing. It is on the cross that Jesus is crucified and becomes a curse so that blessing can come to those who don't have the right by their natural bloodline to be doubly blessed. The cross, when understood properly, can reverse the natural or birth order to God's greater intention and superior spiritual order.

Christ has redeemed us from the curse of the law, having become a curse for us (for it is written, "Cursed is everyone who hangs on a tree"), 14 that the blessing of Abraham might come upon the Gentiles in Christ Jesus, that we might receive the promise of the Spirit through faith. Galatians 3:13-14

Jesus on the cross was a payment and penalty for the sin that Israel had committed against God. Through the curse, those who are near and far, the Jew and the Gentile, have access to Abraham's blessing. But wait; there is something even more powerful we can glean from in this story of adoption.

According to the blessing of Israel upon Ephraim, his seed will become the fullness of the nations. Is this not exactly what the Apostle said in Romans chapter 11 that we read earlier? What Paul preached to the Romans and all who would read was a fulfillment of the blessing given to Ephraim. Through and in Ephraim was a seed that would eventually become the fullness of the nations. The ramifications of this cannot be understated, and when it was a blessing to Joseph and Ephraim, it was certainly a mystery concealed.

Now, we know the rest of the story, for we can see from scriptures how Ephraim, who was called and better known as the house of Israel, rejected the God of their fathers and became worshippers of everything forbidden. In their rebellion they were divorced and scattered among the nations. Yet we read in Romans that it was through their disobedience that God is bringing those very same Gentile nations back with the entire house of Israel, back into the tree and blessing they were divorced from. The fullness of the Gentiles was in the seed of Ephraim who was adopted into Israel. But wait, isn't that what has happened to every believer in Jesus? Are we not all adopted as sons and daughters of God, no matter what nation we are naturally born into?

But when the fullness of the time had come, God sent forth His Son, born of a woman, born under the law, 5 to redeem those who were under the law, that we might receive the adoption as sons. 6 And because you are sons, God has sent forth the Spirit of His Son into your hearts, crying out, "Abba, Father!" 7 Therefore you are no longer a slave but a son, and if a son, then an heir of God through Christ. Galatians 4:4-6

God decided in advance to adopt us into His own family by bringing us to Himself through Jesus Christ. This is what He wanted to do, and it gave Him great pleasure. Ephesians 1:5 NLT

Even to them I will give in My house And within My walls a place and a name Better than that of sons and daughters; I will give them an everlasting name That shall not be cut off. Isaiah 56:5 KJV

The right and privilege of adoption is one of the greatest blessings to those who receive it. The power of adoption is that it legally joins you to a family that you were not naturally born into.

Adoption is a type of grafting into the root and stock of a different tree. With adoption also comes the legal right to inheritances you would not have without it.

We can see that the scriptures teach that all who believe in Jesus as Lord have been adopted now into God's family and are the sons and daughters of God. The adoption gives us rights and privileges and the blessings that come from adoption and virtue of the name bestowed upon us. According to Isaiah, this name given to those adopted is actually a better name than those naturally born. This is because we who are adopted have the double-portion blessing given to Ephraim.

The new covenant blessing is better because the Torah/Word is now written on our hearts though the work of the Holy Spirit. The adoption as sons is one way you receive the blessing and inheritance of Jesus and Abraham. It is how we are forever connected to the fatness of the olive tree. I want you to realize that your identity as a Hebrew Christian gives you a name better than the natural sons and daughters. This is not for you to boast or be proud of, but as a child receive it humbly, for that is the kingdom of God. You are an heir and have an inheritance. Every promise given to physical Israel and Judah can also be claimed as your own. You have been adopted and the blessing though Christ is greater for all who call upon Him.

Now if we are children, then we are heirs--heirs of God and co-heirs with Christ, Romans 8:17a NIV

…he came to save us. Not because of any virtuous deed that
we have done but only because of his extravagant mercy. 6 He
saved us, resurrecting us through the washing of rebirth. We
are made completely new by the Holy Spirit, whom he
splashed over us richly by Jesus, the Messiah, our Life Giver.
7 So as a gift of his love, and since we are faultless—innocent
before his face— we can now become heirs of all things, all
because of an overflowing hope of eternal life. Titus 3:5-7 PT

As we close this chapter, we look forward to completing our journey as we look more closely at the identity that God has made available to anyone who will repent and believe the Gospel.

Chapter Three:

PERSONAL OR GROUP STUDY

1. The process of ____________ has been done for thousands of years. In a sense it connects a _____________ or ________________ to something that has a strong ________ and established foundation.

2. And now your two sons, ___________ and _____________, who were born to you in the land of ___________ before I came to you in Egypt, are _____________; as Reuben and Simeon, they shall be __________. Genesis 48:5

3. Now Israel ___________ the two sons of Egypt and _________ them, if you will, into him.

4. The cross, when understood properly, can ____________ the natural or _____________ order to God's greater intention and superior _____________ order.

5. …that the blessing of _______________ might come upon the _________________ in Christ Jesus, that we might receive the promise of the Spirit through __________. Galatians 3:13-14

6. Through and in ____________ was a seed that would eventually become to be the ____________ of the nations. What does this now mean to you?

____

____

____

____

____

7. But when the _______________ of the time had come, God sent forth His Son, born of a woman, born under the law, 5 to _____________ those who were under the law, that we might receive the ______________as sons. Galatians 4:4-5

8. The power of adoption is that it ______________ joins you to a family that you were not _______________ born into.

9. With adoption also comes the legal right to ___________________ you would not have without it. Describe some things that are now yours in Christ because of the power of being adopted.

10. Your identity as a _______________ Christian gives you a _____________ better than of natural sons and daughters. What does this mean or point to?

____

Chapter Four:

"The Real Gospel"

We have been hacked! The true identity of the believer and disciple of Jesus has been hacked! The bad news is the hack is system (church) wide! The good news is you are now receiving an update and your true identity is in the process of being restored.
We are all in the process of having our identity recovered and restored. The enemy has come to steal your identity away, but Jesus came to restore and give the abundant life that comes from Him.

The sad truth is most people don't even know they have been hacked. They are living in pseudo reality like many in the movie "The Matrix," having their life drained from them while they live in a world that is not even real. The Bible teaches that only when we know the truth can that truth make us free.

The Word of God has many mysteries that are being found "for such a time as this," much like the Torah that was found by Hilkiah and given to young Josiah who, with the heart of a child, began to bring and implement its ways and truth back to Judah and Israel.

Many of you are not familiar with the term Torah unless you have been born Jewish. The Jews know the Torah as the first five books written in the Bible by Moses, also including the other books like the Prophets and Psalms. The word Torah actually has a meaning much more than what most translations inaccurately call law. Torah actually means "instruction" or "to point to with the hand." The root of the word comes from "to throw or shoot." So, Torah is "to hit the mark." It is actually the opposite of the word for sin, which means "to miss the mark." When you obey the word, you "hit the mark." When you don't obey, you sin. It is so simple that we often miss it.

The Torah is not just rules and "dos and don'ts". It is the way to live in the abundant life Jesus taught about, and when you keep the Torah, it is not a burden, but a blessing. Most people think the Torah is outdated and has somehow passed away, but for that to happen, Jesus Himself would have to be outdated and pass away because Jesus is the Torah made flesh. He is the Word and He is always "hitting the mark." He is perfect because He is the Way, the Truth, and the Life.

As you continue in your journey into your identity, you will gradually begin to see that everything God spoke in His Word is to bring us into complete fellowship with God, like Adam had in the Garden before the fall. The Torah will always bring Light to expel the darkness, just like Jesus did as He lived the Torah life. Once the Light exposes the hack, the process of restoring your true identity will begin. You will find yourself free from "The Matrix!" You will begin to see with new vision and you will say like I teach at my church, Save the Nations, "You don't have to do these things, but you get to do them!"

Can you keep a secret? Just kidding. This is one thing I want you to shout from a rooftop. Most Christians do not know what the Gospel is. Now, you are thinking, "Ken, what are you talking about? Everyone knows the Gospel. We have the 'Romans Road,' the 'Wordless Book.' We know what the gospel is! We were taught it in Sunday school."

1. *We are all sinners (Romans 3:23)*
2. *Our righteousness won't save us (Isaiah 64:6)*
3. *God loves everyone (John 3:16)*
4. *Jesus died so we could be made righteous (2 Corinthians 5:21)*
5. *If you believe in Jesus you are saved and have eternal life. (Romans 10:9-10)*

Now, we have scripture for all the five points of the Gospel, right? What if I told you that the Gospel message or story didn't begin in the New Testament, but was actually first preached by God Himself.

And the Scripture, foreseeing that God would justify the Gentiles by faith, preached the gospel to Abraham beforehand, saying, "In you all the nations shall be blessed." 9 So then those who are of faith are blessed with believing Abraham. Galatians 3:8-9 NKJV

Can you see who the first one is to preach the Gospel? It was Yahweh Himself who preached the Gospel to Abraham, the "Gospel" being a proclamation of good news. The Greek understanding of this word gospel is "to announce beforehand something that will happen!" What was God announcing to Abraham at His encounter with Abraham in Genesis chapter 12? He announced His plan of redemption and His plan to graft, or intertwine through Abraham's seed, all the families of the earth. Let's continue to look in the New Testament and see this truth unfold. What is the mystery of the Gospel?

This message was kept secret for centuries and generations past, but now it has been revealed to God's people. 27 For God wanted them to know that the riches and glory of Christ are for you Gentiles, too. And this is the secret: Christ lives in you. This gives you assurance of sharing his glory. Colossians 1:26-27 NLT

God revealed his secret plan and made it known to me. (I have written briefly about this, 4 and if you will read what I have written, you can learn about my understanding of the secret of Christ.) 5 In past times human beings were not told this secret, but God has revealed it now by the Spirit to his holy apostles and prophets. 6 The secret is that by means of the gospel the Gentiles have a part with the Jews in God's blessings; they are members of the same body and share in the promise that God made through Christ Jesus. Ephesians 3:3-6 GNT

In just these two scriptures alone we can see that the Gospel mystery that Paul has been talking about has been largely missed by the Christianity of today. We don't hear much preaching about being "co-heirs" as one translation says. We hear much about the "Gospel of Grace" but we really don't know what it is.

Now all glory to God, who is able to make you strong, just as my Good News says. This message about Jesus Christ has revealed his plan for you Gentiles, a plan kept secret from the beginning of time. Romans 16:25 NLT

For there is no distinction between Jew and Greek; for the same Lord is Lord of all, abounding in riches for all who call on Him; Romans 10:12 NASB (emphasis added)

This righteousness is given through faith in Jesus Christ to all who believe. There is no difference between Jew and Gentile. Romans 3:22 NIV

At the meeting, after long discussion, Peter stood and addressed them as follows: "Brothers, you all know that God chose mefrom among you long ago to preach the Good News to the Gentiles so that they also could believe. 8 God, who knows men's hearts, confirmed the fact that he accepts Gentiles by giving them the Holy Spirit, just as he gave him to us. 9 He made no distinction between them and us, for he cleansed their lives through faith, just as he did ours.
Acts 15:7-9 LB

So Christ came and preached the Good News of peace to all— to you Gentiles, who were far away from God, and to the Jews, who were near to him. 18 It is through Christ that all of us, Jews and Gentiles, are able to come in the one Spirit into the presence of the Father. 19 So then, you Gentiles are not foreigners or strangers any longer; you are now citizens together with God's people and members of the family of God. Ephesians 2:17-19 GNT

- *THE REAL GOSPEL IS WHAT CONNECTS THOSE WHO WERE GENTILES INTO THE INHERITANCE PROMISED TO ABRAHAM*

- *WHEN A PERSON COMES TO FAITH IN CHRIST THEY ARE NO LONGER A GENTILE!*

- *YOU NOW ARE IDENTIFIED AS PART OF THE COMMONWEALTH THAT GOD INTENDED FOR ALL OF ABRAHAM'S SEED AND FOR ALL THE TRIBES OF ISRAEL*

It now time for you to stop saying, "That was for them, Israel or the Jews, but not me." When you accept Christ, you can no longer call yourself a Gentile; no matter to whom or wherever you were born.

We just learned the Word teaches there is no distinction! This is what the Apostle Paul said was the mystery of the Gospel. This is why Jesus came; not just so we don't go to hell, but that we get to have the richness of the heritage that God promised to Abraham. "All the families" means "all those who believe in Jesus" get the blessings of Abraham and all the promises given to Israel and his sons, which also includes the adopted sons from Egypt, Ephraim and Manasseh.

For neither being circumcised nor being uncircumcised matters; what matters is being a new creation. 16 And as many as order their lives by this rule, shalom upon them and mercy, and upon the Israel of God! Galatians 6:15-16 CJB

The Apostle Paul was not against circumcision. What he was against was the people making circumcision (works) the determining factor for salvation rather than faith and grace. Paul was fighting those who could not accept Gentiles coming into their inheritance by faith. They wanted them to go through man-made, rabbinic conversion rather than Christ.

When you understand you are now a part of and connected to Israel, you begin to understand why it is important to honor the biblical traditions that God gave to give revelation and application to your life when you follow Jesus Christ. Please know that the church does not and never will replace the Jew or Israel. This is a false doctrine that has been used to teach and demonstrate hatred, murder and war against God's people.

As we close this chapter, remember that the Gospel means "good news." It is the Gospel of Grace that brings people into an inheritance and family that they were previously disconnected from or had no legal right to. The mystery of the Gospel goes even deeper when we understand who Jesus was, a Kinsman Redeemer who actually came to redeem us, and how the mercy, love and righteousness of God will be manifested to those who need it most.

Chapter Four:

PERSONAL OR GROUP STUDY

1. The enemy has come to steal your ______________ away, but Jesus came to ______________ and give the abundant life that comes from Him.

2. Torah actually means ______________ or "to point to with the hand." The root of the word comes from "to throw" or "shoot." So, Torah is "to _______ the ________."

3. This message was kept secret for centuries and generations past, but now it has been ______________ to God's people. 27 For God wanted them to know that the _________ and glory of Christ are for you ____________, too. And this is the ____________: Christ lives in you. This gives you assurance of sharing his glory. Colossians 1:26-27 NLT

4. The secret is that by means of the gospel the ____________ have a part with the Jews in God's blessings; they are members of the _______ body and share in the ____________ that God made through Christ Jesus. Ephesians 3:6 GNT

5. For there is no____________ between Jew and Greek; for the same Lord is Lord of all, abounding in riches for all who call on Him; Romans 10:12 NASB

6. When someone comes to faith in Jesus they are no longer a ________________.

7. It is the Gospel of ___________ that brings people into an ____________________ and family that they were previously disconnected from or had no ____________ right to.

8. What is the true gospel and what does it mean for Christians today?

____

____

____

____

____

____

____

9. So then, you _________ are not foreigners or strangers any ____________; you are now citizens __________ with God's people and members of the family of God. Ephesians 2:19 GNT

Chapter Five:

Torah's Triplets

It is the glory of God to conceal a matter,
But the glory of kings is to search out a matter.
Proverbs 25:2

In Matthew chapter 23, Jesus makes a profound statement. We must learn how to mine and search the scriptures for the gold that is found in them. This is what kings are to do!

"Woe to you, scribes and Pharisees, hypocrites! For you pay tithe of mint and anise and cummin, and have neglected the weightier matters of the law: justice and mercy and faith. These you ought to have done, without leaving the others undone. Matthew 23:23 NKJV

I like to call the three things Jesus says are the weightier matters of the law as "God's or Torah's Triplets." We can begin by understanding that justice, mercy and faith have been, and always will be connected to the Torah. God is and has always been a God that demands justice, has great mercy, and is only pleased by faith. We must realize that God cannot give mercy without justice, nor can He require faith without an action of obedience.

The mission God had for Israel was to be a light to the nations. This is why He gave them the Torah. He wanted them to demonstrate and share with the nations on how to "hit the mark" and walk with Yahweh God. But "Houston, we have a problem." Israel so far has failed their mission. Instead of being a light, they have become full of darkness themselves, embracing the gods and ways of the nations.

When Israel wanted a king, Saul was chosen and looked the part, being tall and handsome. Unfortunately, his qualities were only skin deep, so the kingdom was torn from him and given to David, a man after God's heart and one who would carry out God's will.

And when He had removed him, He raised up for them David as king, to whom also He gave testimony and said, 'I have found David the son of Jesse, a man after My own heart, who will do all My will.' Acts 13:22 NKJV

David made mistakes, but was quick to repent. He was a humble man who was not ashamed to worship and to obey God's Word. David ruled over all the tribes of Israel, but his son, Solomon did not follow in David's ways.

Solomon started out right, but like so many, his great success became a snare to him. He forgot and rejected the God who gave him the wisdom and the wealth. He worshipped the gods of his many wives who from the nations the Lord told Israel not to marry.

Because of David's faithfulness, God promised that Judah and Jerusalem would always have a light and a future kingdom. Even when at a later time Judah would go into apostasy, the promise and covenant to David and His sons would stand forever. (2 Kings 8:19, 2 Chronicles 21:7)

Solomon refuses to repent and rejects the God who appears to him twice. God had told him that the kingdom would be torn from him and only one tribe would be with Judah in Jerusalem, but Solomon does not humble himself and will not receive God's mercy. Before judgment was pronounced God gave Solomon a warning but nowhere does he even remotely say he is sorry or repent for his idolatry and rebellion to God's Torah instruction. Instead He misses the mark completely, which is the definition of sin in both the Hebrew and the Greek.

A prophet comes to one of the servants of Solomon, Jeroboam, and speaks these words:

Now it happened at that time, when Jeroboam went out of Jerusalem, that the prophet Ahijah the Shilonite met him on the way; and he had clothed himself with a new garment, and the two were alone in the field. 30 Then Ahijah took hold of the new garment that was on him, and tore it into twelve pieces. 31 And he said to Jeroboam, "Take for yourself ten pieces, for thus says the Lord, the God of Israel: 'Behold, I will tear the kingdom out of the hand of Solomon and will give ten tribes to you 32 (but he shall have one tribe for the sake of My servant David, and for the sake of Jerusalem, the city which I have chosen out of all the tribes of Israel), 33 because they have a forsaken Me, and worshiped Ashtoreth the goddess of the Sidonians, Chemosh the god of the Moabites, and Milcom the god of the people of Ammon, and have not walked in My ways to do what is right in My eyes and keep My statutes and My judgments, as did his father David. 34 However I will not take the whole kingdom out of his hand, because I have made him ruler all the days of his life for the sake of My servant David, whom I chose because he kept My commandments and My statutes. 35 But I will take the kingdom out of his son's hand and give it to you—ten tribes. 36 And to his son I will give one tribe, that My servant David may always have a lamp before Me in Jerusalem, the city which I have chosen for Myself, to put My name there. 37 So I will take you, and you shall reign over all your heart desires, and you shall be king over Israel. 38 Then it shall be, if you heed all that I command you, walk in My ways, and do what is right in My sight, to keep My statutes and My commandments, as My servant David did, then I will be with you and build for you an enduring house, as I built for David, and will give Israel to you. 39 And I will afflict the descendants of David because of this, but not forever.'" 1 Kings 11:29-39 NKJV

After Solomon's death, this prophetic act of tearing the kingdom comes to pass as Rehoboam, Solomon's son, in his pride causes this word to be fulfilled. The division of the Southern and Northern Kingdoms divides, for the most part, Ephraim, known as the house of Israel with the ten tribes to the North, and the House of Judah with Benjamin in the south. Jeroboam does not want his people to go to Jerusalem where the temple is to worship, so he builds altars and places golden calves in Dan and in Bethel. He tells them "It's too far to go to Jerusalem," and then makes some new feast days similar, but at different times than the feast days God gave for all those tribes who were present at Mount Sinai after crossing over from Egypt. God warned Jeroboam and the kings of the house of Israel that would follow of what would happen if they continued to disobey. In fact, Moses gave them all this warning:

"Remember the instruction you gave your servant Moses, saying, 'If you are unfaithful, I will scatter you among the nations, Nehemiah 1:8 NIV

I call heaven and earth to witness against you this day, that you will soon utterly perish from the land which you cross over the Jordan to possess; you will not prolong your days in it, but will be utterly destroyed. 27 And the Lord will scatter you among the peoples, and you will be left few in number among the nations where the Lord will drive you. 28 And there you will serve gods, the work of men's hands, wood and stone, which neither see nor hear nor eat nor smell. 29 But from there you will seek the Lord your God, and you will find Him if you seek Him with all your heart and with all your soul. 30 When you are in distress, and all these things come upon you in the latter days, when you turn to the Lord your God and obey His voice 31 (for the Lord your God is a merciful God), He will not forsake you nor destroy you, nor forget the covenant of your fathers which He swore to them.

Deuteronomy 4:26-30 NKJV

We can see that God with His mercy wants them to return and obey the Lord, but the consequences of their disobedience will cause their eventual scattering among the nations. This is what happened specifically and eventually to the Northern House of Israel between the years 740-722 B.C. they were carried into captivity to Assyria and never to return again as a kingdom.

Nevertheless they would not hear, but stiffened their necks, like the necks of their fathers, who did not believe in the Lord their God. 15 And they rejected His statutes and His covenant that He had made with their fathers, and His testimonies which He had testified against them; they followed idols, became idolaters, and went after the nations who were all around them, concerning whom the Lord had charged them that they should not do like them. 16 So they left all the commandments of the Lord their God, made for themselves a molded image and two calves, made a wooden image and worshiped all the host of heaven, and served Baal. 17 And they caused their sons and daughters to pass through the fire, practiced witchcraft and soothsaying, and sold themselves to do evil in the sight of the Lord, to provoke Him to anger. 18 Therefore the Lord was very angry with Israel, and removed them from His sight; there was none left but the tribe of Judah alone.19 Also Judah did not keep the commandments of the Lord their God, but walked in the statutes of Israel which they made. 20 And the Lord rejected all the descendants of Israel, afflicted them, and delivered them into the hand of plunderers, until He had cast them from His sight. 21 For He tore Israel from the house of David, and they made Jeroboam the son of Nebat king. Then Jeroboam drove Israel from following the Lord, and made them commit a great sin. 22 For the children of Israel walked in all the sins of Jeroboam which he did; they did not depart from them, 23 until the Lord removed Israel out of His sight, as He had said by all His servants the prophets. So Israel was carried away from their own land to Assyria, as it is to this day. 2 Kings 17:14-19 NKJV

Now, the lost tribes of Israel have been a hot topic, particularly for me when I was in Hebrew school preparing for my Bar- Mitzvah. We know from the scriptures that the House of Israel was swallowed up and scattered among the Gentiles. Remember Judah, because of David, was promised to always be a lamp and to have a future king. This is one of the reasons that Messiah, Yeshua-Jesus will be born to the tribe of Judah, fulfilling God's covenant promise to David.

The house of Israel, however, was given a letter of divorce and legally they could not be restored to their former glory and heritage… or could they? According to the Word they have been scattered as lost sheep among the nations. Could these be the sheep that Jesus was talking about in John chapter 10 as the ones He would gather and bring home? If the house of Israel is the "lost sheep," then how can this be done, satisfying God's Torah Triplets of justice, mercy and faith? How can God bring home a people who rejected their own identity and forfeited their inheritance? Could, even in their rebellion, God still have a plan and a way that would not only bring them back, but to include the Gentile nations where they now lived?

Israel is swallowed up; Now they are among the Gentiles Like a vessel in which is no pleasure. 9 For they have gone up to Assyria, Like a wild donkey alone by itself; Ephraim has hired lovers. 10 Yes, though they have hired among the nations, Now I will gather them; And they shall sorrow a little, Because of the burden of the king of princes. 11 "Because Ephraim has made many altars for sin, They have become for him altars for sinning. 12 I have written for him the great things of My law, But they were considered a strange thing. Hosea 8:8-12 NKJV

"Israel is like scattered sheep; The lions have driven him away Jeremiah 50:17 NKJV

As a shepherd seeks out his flock on the day he is among his scattered sheep, so will I seek out My sheep and deliver them from all the places where they were scattered on a cloudy and dark day. Ezekiel 34:12 NKJV

Then they despised the pleasant land; They did not believe His word, 25 But complained in their tents, And did not heed the voice of the Lord. 26 Therefore He raised His hand in an oath against them, To overthrow them in the wilderness, 27 To overthrow their descendants among the nations, And to scatter them in the lands. 28 They joined themselves also to Baal of Peor, And ate sacrifices made to the dead. 29 Thus they provoked Him to anger with their deeds, And the plague broke out among them. 30 Then Phinehas stood up and intervened, And the plague was stopped. 31 And that was accounted to him for righteousness To all generations

forevermore. 32 They angered Him also at the waters of strife,
So that it went ill with Moses on account of them; 33 Because
they rebelled against His Spirit, So that he spoke rashly with
his lips. 34 They did not destroy the peoples, Concerning
whom the Lord had commanded them, 35 But they mingled
with the Gentiles And learned their works; 36 They served
their idols, Which became a snare to them. 37 They even
sacrificed their sons And their daughters to demons, 38 And
shed innocent blood, The blood of their sons and daughters,
Whom they sacrificed to the idols of Canaan; And the land
was polluted with blood. 39 Thus they were defiled by their
own works, And played the harlot by their own deeds. 40
Therefore the wrath of the Lord was kindled against His
people, So that He abhorred His own inheritance. 41 And He
gave them into the hand of the Gentiles, And those who hated
them ruled over them. 42 Their enemies also oppressed them,
And they were brought into subjection under their hand. 43
Many times He delivered them; But they rebelled in their
counsel, And were brought low for their iniquity. 44
Nevertheless He regarded their affliction, When He heard
their cry; 45 And for their sake He remembered His covenant,
And relented according to the multitude of His mercies. 46 He
also made them to be pitied By all those who carried them
away captive. 47 Save us, O Lord our God, And gather us
from among the Gentiles, To give thanks to Your holy name,
To triumph in Your praise.48 Blessed be the Lord God of
Israel From everlasting to everlasting! And let all the people
say, "Amen!" Praise the Lord! Psalm 106:24-48

“For surely I will command, And will sift the house of Israel among all nations, As grain is sifted in a sieve; Yet not the smallest grain shall fall to the ground. Amos 9:9

If we continue reading Amos chapter 9 we find a promise that is quoted in the book of Acts about the Gentiles being saved as part of God’s plan.

“On that day I will raise up the tabernacle of David, which has fallen down, and repair its damages; I will raise up its ruins, and rebuild it as in the days of old; 12 That they may possess the remnant of Edom, and all the Gentiles who are called by My name,” Says the Lord who does this thing. Amos 9:11-12

Then all the multitude kept silent and listened to Barnabas and Paul declaring how many miracles and wonders God had worked through them among the Gentiles. 13 And after they had become silent, James answered, saying, “Men and brethren, listen to me: 14 Simon has declared how God at the first visited the Gentiles to take out of them a people for His name. 15 And with this the words of the prophets agree, just as it is written: 16 ‘After this I will return And will rebuild the tabernacle of David, which has fallen down; I will rebuild its ruins, And I will set it up; 17 So that the rest of mankind may seek the Lord, Even all the Gentiles who are called by My name, Says the Lord who does all these things.
Acts 15:12-17 NKJV

The prophecy from the book of Amos points to the scattered of the house Israel that would return to God and bring with them the Gentile nations. In a sense, the house of

Israel had become married to those nations and their gods. Their identity was swallowed up and lost. They too had been hacked by rejecting and being unfaithful to their first Husband, who was Yahweh God.

The story is not over, for in their rejection an open door, according to Romans chapter 11, has come until the fullness of the nations comes to Christ. If we read Romans chapter 11, we will see that the Apostle Paul is referring the nation of Israel as having been broken off from the very olive tree that now supports those who were Gentile believers. It is also obvious that God's plan from the beginning of the prophecy and blessings over Ephraim is that the gospel would come to the Gentile nations. Just like He also told the father of our faith, Abraham, about in his seed (Christ) all families of the earth would be grafted and intertwined into the covenant promises and blessings.

Finally, in order to do this, we know that God's Triplets all must be satisfied. How can God give mercy without justice and require an act of faith? God, in His Torah, has a law and a potential curse for those who are divorced because of unfaithfulness.

"When a man takes a wife and marries her, and it happens that she finds no favor in his eyes because he has found some uncleanness in her, and he writes her a certificate of divorce, puts it in her hand, and sends her out of his house, 2 when she has departed from his house, and goes and becomes another man's wife, 3 if the latter husband detests her and writes her a certificate of divorce, puts it in her hand, and sends her out of his house, or if the latter husband dies who took her as his wife, 4 then her former husband who divorced her must not take her back to be his wife after she has been defiled; for that is an abomination before the Lord, and you shall not bring sin on the land which the Lord your God is giving you as an inheritance. Deuteronomy 24:1-4 NKJV

- *ACCORDING TO THE TORAH LAW IT IS IMPOSSIBLE FOR A DIVORCED WOMAN TO GO BACK TO HER FIRST HUSBAND AFTER SHE HAS REMARRIED, EVEN IF HER NEW HUSBAND DIES.*

Then I saw that for all the causes for which backsliding Israel had committed adultery, I had put her away and given her a certificate of divorce; yet her treacherous sister Judah did not fear, but went and played the harlot also. Jeremiah 3:8

God has given to the house of Israel for their constant unfaithfulness a letter of divorce. The book of Hosea depicts Hosea as God and Gomer as a harlot like Israel. It is in Hosea that Israel will lose their heritage and their identity as a covenant people. They will mix themselves with the nations and lose everything, yet even in this story God continually speaks of mercy. Remember all three of God's Triplets must somehow be satisfied. There must be justice, mercy and faith. Since the house of Israel is now divorced, according to the Torah they can never go back to their first Husband, Yahweh.

Ephraim is stricken, Their root is dried up; They shall bear no fruit. Yes, were they to bear children, I would kill the darlings of their womb." 17 My God will cast them away, Because they did not obey Him; And they shall be wanderers among the nations. Hosea 9:16-17 NKJV

God, because of his mercy and unfailing love, has promised over and over in His Word that He will be reunited to the house of Israel, the lost and scattered, and yes, now remarried people to the gods of the nations!

"They say, 'If a man divorces his wife, And she goes from him And becomes another man's, May he return to her again?' Would not that land be greatly polluted? But you have played the harlot with many lovers; Yet return to Me," says the Lord. 14 "Return, O backsliding children," says the Lord; "for I am married to you. I will take you, one from a city and two from a family, and I will bring you to Zion 20 Surely, as a wife treacherously departs from her husband, So have you dealt treacherously with Me, O house of Israel," says the Lord. Jeremiah 3:1, 14, 20 NKJV

The mystery of the gospel had been hidden from even those prophets who spoke these words. After Jesus rose from the dead He opens the disciples' understanding to the scriptures that were all written about Him. He tells them it was necessary for Messiah to suffer and rise on the third day and to preach in His name to all nations.

Then He said to them, "These are the words which I spoke to you while I was still with you, that all things must be fulfilled which were written in the Law of Moses and the Prophets and the Psalms concerning Me." 45 And He opened their understanding, that they might comprehend the Scriptures. 46

Then He said to them, "Thus it is written, and thus it was necessary for the Christ to suffer and to rise from the dead the third day, 47 and that repentance and remission of sins should be preached in His name to all nations, beginning at Jerusalem. 48 And you are witnesses of these things. 49 Behold, I send the Promise of My Father upon you; but tarry in the city of Jerusalem until you are endued with power from on high." Luke 24:44-49

It was necessary for Christ to suffer and to rise from the dead! You see, Jesus, representing the tribe of Judah, was going to be the Kinsman Redeemer, for only a kinsman had the right to redeem another tribe's inheritance. For Him to do that He had to deal with the justice that was required, and the penalty for the house of Israel's rebellion was the price of blood. This was an act of mercy by God Himself as the One who sent His only begotten Son who was sent on a mission from heaven to seek and to save that which was lost. The lost sheep would be found and restored to the fold, but not until the Shepherd would give His life as a ransom and price of redemption. So why did Jesus have to be raised from the dead? It was to satisfy the Law of Divorce, which said you couldn't remarry the first husband after you have been polluted or put away, even if your present husband is now dead. This is the curse of the law that the Apostle Paul is actually talking about in Galatians that has decreed that fallen house of Israel is now cutoff and under a curse. They have lost their identity and inheritance among the gentiles. It would seem that they were willingly hacked by their blatant adultery and idolatry and were mixed among the nations. Their inheritance is still intact, but it is no longer in their reach for they are all under a curse that cuts them off from what was their inheritance. They are like the younger brother in the story of the prodigal son who the Father says was dead when He lost everything and ended up eating with the swine. The father in the end of the story goes to meet not a servant but a son who the Father will restore to a place even better than when the younger son left home. The prodigal son parable is really a story of the older brother representing the house of Judah and the younger brother representing the house of Ephraim. In the end God will somehow bring his lost sheep home and give them by grace more than they could ever work for or earn. Now let's look at what the Apostle Paul really meant in the book of Romans. They mystery will now be revealed to those who have ears to hear.

Or do you not know, brethren (for I speak to those who know the law), that the law has dominion over a man as long as he lives? 2 For the woman who has a husband is bound by the law to her husband as long as he lives. But if the husband dies, she is released from the law of her husband. 3 So then if, while her husband lives, she marries another man, she will be called an adulteress; but if her husband dies, she is free from that law, so that she is no adulteress, though she has married another man. 4 Therefore, my brethren, you also have become dead to the law through the body of Christ, that you may be married to another—to Him who was raised from the dead, that we should bear fruit to God. Romans 7:1-4 NKJV (emphasis added)

Jesus died to free Israel from the Law of Divorce and sinful adultery. This is why Jesus had to die on the cross and

become and take the curse and reproach of divorce away from the House of Israel who became gentiles and married the nations.
When Jesus died Israel was no longer a divorced woman. She could now remarry, however she still could not come back and marry Yahweh God, or could she? She was now free from the law of divorce. Jesus death was the payment for all the sin, which included the rebellion, idolatry and marriage to the ways and gods of the nations that the house of Ephraim had committed. Is it possible that when Jesus died we identify with that death and we die too? When Jesus is buried are we not buried with Him? When He is raised are we not also raised to new life as new people?

Jesus death solved one half of the problem; the Torah law said that even though the husband was dead, she could not re-marry the first husband since she was defiled. Jesus, with justice, mercy and faith, solved this when He rose from the dead a New Man (bridegroom) and eligible to marry a new virtuous woman (bride). This is the greatest of all love stories! Wrapped up in the death, burial and resurrection of Jesus is how God's Triplets of justice, mercy and faith will bring the fallen house of Ephraim and the gentiles into a new covenant with Yahweh God through the grace and truth of the only one who could connect and marry those who had formerly been gentiles either by birth or by being cut off and scattered among the nations.

The next time you read Ephesians chapter 5 about marriage, read it with the greater understanding that Christ left His Father in heaven to reunite God with a new bride that was previously married to sin and the world. He leaves heaven on a mission to restore a relationship that would require the His suffering and death to redeem with mercy an unworthy bride.

Jesus suffered by shedding innocent blood. His death is the full payment for Israel's rebellion, idolatry and adultery. Jesus' blood & death also satisfies the laws demand that the divorced woman cannot remarry. The only way for Israel to remarry Yahweh and have the covenant renewed is through Christ. Yeshua is the way they are grafted-in as branches again to the olive tree's inheritance and blessing. So now we can see that all of God's Torah Triplets are now satisfied. We see perfect justice, mercy and faith all working together to fulfill God's prophetic Word.

Both the Bride/the house of Israel and the bridegroom, Jesus from the house of Judah were both made into One New Man! Just like in natural marriage you become one flesh, in Christ you become one in spirit. There are no barriers of sin, the past, the old man or life to hold us captive or keep us from a new future.

Christ has redeemed us from the curse of the law, having become a curse for us (for it is written, "Cursed is everyone who hangs on a tree"). Galatians 3:13

Jesus satisfies the curse of the Law of Divorce against us with His death and suffering with blood, but the resurrection qualifies Him to re-marry His first love! In doing this, Jesus operates in God's Torah Triplets of justice, mercy and faith. It will take faith for "whosever will" to call on the name of the

Lord to be saved. It is through faith we access the grace, mercy and righteousness that only comes from what Jesus alone came on a mission to do.

Jesus came to seek and save the lost sheep of the house of Israel, but in His death and resurrection He made it possible for people from every nation to access the blessings and privilege of the covenant. The covenant was given to Abraham and then re-confirmed through Moses and the Prophets. The new covenant was given to the house of Israel because they are the ones who broke their marriage vows. The mystery of the Gospel reunites, through Jesus' resurrection, all who are lost and without hope. By the way this is what is happening in Ezekiel 37 in the story of the dry bones of the house of Israel, they were dead and cut off, but in the end they will have God's breath blow like the wind and will be born again and become a mighty army.

When Jesus teaches on Torah's Triplets, He is using a technique called hinting. Jesus hints at the divorce of the house of Israel when He uses the word "omit," which actually means "to divorce." He was telling the Pharisees not to divorce the weightier matters of the law, which are justice, mercy and faith. The lost sheep of the house of Israel had their identity hacked, but it is now being restored into an even better one than they had before. Because now they will have the Torah written on there hearts and will have an intimacy with Yahweh in a marriage that makes them One like Jesus prayed in John chapter seventeen.

Because finding fault with them, He says: "Behold, the days are coming, says the Lord, when I will make a new covenant with the house of Israel and with the house of Judah— 9 not according to the covenant that I made with their fathers in the day when I took them by the hand to lead them out of the land of Egypt; because they did not continue in My covenant, and I disregarded them, says the Lord. 10 For this is the covenant that I will make with the house of Israel after those days, says the Lord: I will put My laws in their mind and write them on their hearts; and I will be their God, and they shall be My people. 11 None of them shall teach his neighbor, and none his brother, saying, 'Know the Lord,' for all shall know Me, from the least of them to the greatest of them. 12 For I will be merciful to their unrighteousness, and their sins and their lawless deed I will remember no more." Hebrews 8:8-12

Do you see whom the new covenant is actually for? It is for the house of Israel who broke and gotten divorced from through idolatry and the sins of the nations. It is interesting that for years we heard many people talk of being a "New Testament" or "Covenant" church, but never heard them talk of who the covenant was actually given to. It wasn't made with Christians; it was made with the house of Israel and Judah. The reason it is new is because the gentiles who would be grafted in to the house of Israel never had a covenant in the first place.

The covenant is new and better because it is Jesus, from the house of Judah, who has guaranteed it as its King, Priest and Mediator. This is the covenant we get to be included in. Hallelujah! Thank God for His Triplets of justice, mercy and faith. There was never a problem with the covenant or the Torah. The fault was found with them who were rebellious and unfaithful. These are those who were without hope.

…that at that time you were without Christ, being aliens from the commonwealth of Israel and strangers from the covenants of promise, having no hope and without God in the world. 13 But now in Christ Jesus you who once were far off have been brought near by the blood of Christ. Ephesians 2:12-13NKJV

Now look at this promise to Israel in Hosea, then guess where we find it written in the New Testament, and who do you think gets the benefits of it?

Now when she had weaned Lo-Ruhamah, she conceived and bore a son. 9 Then God said "Call his name Lo-Ammi, For you are not My people, And I will not be your God. 10 "Yet the number of the children of Israel Shall be as the sand of the sea, Which cannot be measured or numbered. And it shall come to pass In the place where it was said to them, 'You are not My people,' There it shall be said to them, You are sons of the living God.' 11 Then the children of Judah and the children of Israel Shall be gathered together, And appoint for themselves one head; And they shall come up out of the land, For great will be the day of Jezreel! Hosea 1: 8-11 NKJV

This scripture is spoken over the house of Israel who, like Gomer the Harlot, is unfaithful to her husband. The son that she conceived was named Lo-Ammi which meant "For you are not My people, And I will not be your God." The son was to be a sign for Israel that they have lost their heritage and

God. But immediately afterwards, God, in His mercy, promises those same people that they will become sons of the living God and will be fully restored to their brothers in the house of Judah. In Romans chapter 9 the Apostle Paul tells us that in Hosea God is speaking, not just of the house of Israel, but the Gentiles. (Romans 9:25-26)

God's plan was always to bring the Gentiles into covenant. This is the mystery of the gospel. Even Peter quotes the same scripture in Hosea and applies it to the new identity of former Gentiles.

But you are a chosen generation, a royal priesthood, a holy nation, His own special people, that you may proclaim the praises of Him who called you out of darkness into His marvelous light; 10 who once were not a people but are now the people of God, who had not obtained mercy but now have obtained mercy. 1 Peter 2:9-10 NKJV

Thank God for His Torah's Triplets of justice, mercy and faith. It is time for you to fully embrace the download from heaven and remember to get the updates. The Holy Spirit is the one who will teach you what is of the truth. Jesus said that those who know truth will hear His voice.

I believe the scriptures are very clear on our identity when we are born again. God is not trying to make you Jewish, but remember you are married to Jesus from Judah "A JEW!" That is why I like to call myself a Hebrew Christian. I have "crossed over" from Egypt and the world systems into a covenant relationship with the one true God. Like Abraham, we are “crossed-over ones.” We have passed from darkness to light, from death to life, from sin to righteousness, from sickness to health, from poverty to blessing, and from brokenness into God’s Peace. The Shalom that Jesus came to bring will leave us in a better place than before. His Shalom is “Nothing Missing, Nothing Broken, Nothing Lost, All Restored!” This is the blessing you are now blessed with!

And the Lord spoke to Moses, saying: 23 “Speak to Aaron and his sons, saying, ‘This is the way you shall bless the children of Israel. Say to them 24 “The Lord bless you and keep you; 25 The Lord make His face shine upon you, and be gracious to you; 26 The Lord lift up His countenance upon you, and give you peace. (shalom)”’ 27 “So they shall put My name on the children of Israel, and I will bless them.” Numbers 6:22-27 NKJV

You are no longer hacked you have a rich inheritance and now you know who you are. God wants you to live from this foundation. You are a Hebrew Christian and are living free from the curse of the law having received the spirit of God you are now born again into a rich stock and family that has a legacy for you now and for your future. It is time for us as Hebrew Christians to make natural Israel and the Jewish people jealous and provoke them by living in the light of the Torah as an example and manifestation of sons and daughters but also as those who are now married to the Lord. I hope you received this teaching and can say I am a Hebrew Christian, Abraham is the father of my faith and I am forever connected to Israel and to Jesus my Messiah and kinsmen redeemer.

Chapter Five:

PERSONAL OR GROUP STUDY

1. "Woe to you, scribes and Pharisees, hypocrites! For you pay tithe of mint and anise and cummin, and have neglected the weightier matters of the law: _________ and ___________ and ________________. These you ought to have done, without leaving the others undone. Matthew 23:23 NKJV

2. We must realize that God cannot give __________ without justice, nor can He require _______________ without an action of ________________.

3. The mission God had for _____________ was to be a light to the _____________. This is why He gave them the _________.

4. But I will take the _____________ out of his son's hand and give it to you—______ tribes. 36 And to his son I will give one tribe, that My servant ___________ may always have a _____________ before Me in ______________, the city which I have chosen for Myself, to put My name there. 1 Kings 11:35-36

5. "Remember the _______________ you gave your servant Moses, saying, 'If you are unfaithful, I will _____________ you among the nations, Nehemiah 1:8 NIV

6. And with this the words of the _____________ agree, just as it is written: 16 'After this I will return And will rebuild the tabernacle of David, which has fallen down; I will rebuild its ruins, And I will set it up; 17 So that the rest of ________________ may seek the Lord, Even all the _______________ who are called by My __________, Says the Lord who does all these things. Acts 15:15-17 NKJV

7. According to the _____________it is impossible for a divorced woman to go back to her first ____________ after she has remarried, even if her new husband ____________.

8. Since the house of Israel is now ____________, according to the _____________ they can never go _________ to their first Husband, Yahweh.

9. And He opened their understanding, that they might comprehend the __________________. 46 Then He said to them, "Thus it is _______________, and thus it was necessary for the Christ to _____________ and to _____________ from the dead the ________ day, 47 and that repentance and remission of sins should be preached in His name to all ______________, beginning at Jerusalem. Luke 24:45-47

10. Jesus satisfies the curse of the Law of _____________ against us with His death and suffering with blood, but the ______________ qualifies Him to re-marry His first love! In

doing this, Jesus operates in God's ___________ of justice, mercy and faith.

AFTERWORD

I hope that you have learned something that will help you discern the plan and purposes of God for your life but also for all people. God and His Word are good! His intentions as we walk in His plan are always to bless us. The fall of man in the Garden of Eden did not catch God by surprise. God had already slain the Lamb of God before the creation. He knew and by His sovereignty provided a way back to the Garden for all mankind. The light of the gospel and mystery of grace is how God can take a fallen man or cut off tribe like the House of Israel and bring them back by giving them covenant through His messiah Jesus. The back-story of how God does this is the demonstration of His wisdom and great love. If you were born a gentile remember that Jesus has connected you to Israel and the covenant of Abraham. The church of Jesus is a fulfillment of God's promise to Abraham that in His seed all the families and the Nations would come into blessing as part of His seed. In 1 Chronicles chapter five we find that the birthright blessing is passed to the sons of Joseph who were adopted by Israel but Judah will prevail and descend the ruler. Jesus is that ruler and Messiah who will restore to Israel's sons known as the House of Israel their birthright. The blessing over them was that in them would be the fullness of the Nations. What a mystery, what a story of redemption. Anyone who comes to Jesus gets connected to the covenant God made with the House of Judah and the House of Israel. The way you get connected is by faith in Jesus. After you confess and receive Him you will then begin to walk out the ways of the Torah. This is to be done by the Helper who is the Holy Spirit who will lead and guide you as you seek God, read His Word and ask for His guidance and direction. Ask Him to teach you His ways. He will help you Hit the Mark for that is what God has always intended by His Torah. If you want to know more about this and how to walk this out please read my next book in this series called: "Hit the Mark". It will answer many hard questions while also take what you learned from this foundational teaching and show you what to do next as God leads of course. If you enjoyed and learned something in this book, please share it with someone you love or care about. Remember you are no longer hacked, you are a Hebrew Christian.

Kenneth S. Albin

About the Author

Kenneth "Ken" Albin was born in New York, but moved to Florida as a young seven-year-old. Shortly after moving, Ken's parents were divorced, which left him deeply hurt for many years. During this time Ken, being Jewish, went to Hebrew school and Temple regularly. At the time of his thirteenth birthday and Bar Mitzvah, many confirmed a calling as a "rabbi" or "cantor" on his life.

It was soon after this that Ken's grandparents met the Lord at a Full Gospel businessmen's meeting. With momentum that came from above, Ken's father, David accepted the Lord, Jesus as his Savior. Being moved by his father's "born again" experience, Ken was now himself open to hear the message that so radically changed his dad's life. In the summer of Ken's sophomore year of high school, he gave his life to Jesus and his life was radically altered. He has been faithful to the house of God ever since. His mother, Racquel had also accepted Jesus and was now serving the Lord full time in Messianic ministry with her new husband, Rabbi Charles Kluge.

Ken has served in various areas of ministry including children's ministry, youth ministry and music ministry. He also has served in both associate and senior pastor roles for over twenty years. He has earned his Bachelor of Theology from International Seminary and his Master's Degree from Liberty University. He is also an accomplished singer/songwriter who has written over 100 songs. He loves to worship with the guitar and the keyboard.

Ken met his wife, Lisa at her grandfather's church in Margate, Florida. They were married when Lisa was just eighteen years of age. Six years later they welcomed their only child, Brittney into the world. Today Brittney and her husband, A.J. serve with Ken and Lisa in ministry and have a beautiful daughter, Brielle.

Ken and Lisa founded Save the Nations Church along with a handful of committed people who gathered in a home on September 17, 2006. God had put a vision in their hearts to reach the nations and bring light to a hurting world. Ken and Lisa currently serve as the overseeing pastors of the South Florida church campus in Broward County. As founders and pastors, they desire to inspire, instruct, resource and help people discover the destiny God has for them. The nations have become their home as together they travel to the nations, teaching, reviving and sharing the resources that help make influential disciples and bring people into appreciation of God's Torah, His "instructions."

Ken has always preached the word with the inspiration and revelation of the Holy Spirit. He has recently been on a journey to bring Christians into an understanding of the roots of their faith. "The Christian church has been hacked!" as Ken states in one of his latest books about restoring the inheritance and identity back to the church.

Presently, there are two international Save the Nations churches in Brazil: one in Rio and one in Marica'. Brazilian pastors, Diego and Kelly are doing an amazing work for God and great fruit is seen in that nation.

Ken has authored many books. All are available on Amazon. They are also being translated to Spanish, Portuguese and Russian languages.

BOOKS BY KENNETH S. ALBIN

YOU ARE BORN FOR THE EXTRAORDINARY

UPSIDE OF DOWN

THE MYSTERY OF THE CROWN

HACKED: THE HEBREW CHRISTIAN

CHRISTIANS GET TO CELEBRATE PASSOVER TOO!

NO MORE LEAVEN

HIT THE MARK

HIDDEN BLESSINGS REVEALED

TABERNACLES IT'S A CELEBRATION & NOT JUST AN OPTION!

HANUKKAH AND PURIM ARE FOR CHRISTIANS TOO

Contact Information: for Ken & Lisa Albin
www.savethenations.com / www.hitthemarktorah.tv
info@savethenations.com

THE BLESSINGS OF PENTECOST

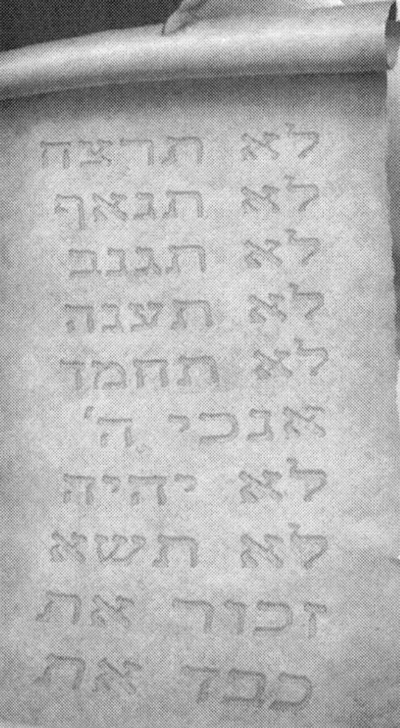

KENNETH S. ALBIN

CÓMO YENDO INTENCIONALMENTE HACIA ABAJO PODEMOS TOMAR ALTURA

MENGUANDO para CRECER

PREFACIO:
DR. MARK CHIRONNA

KENNETH S. ALBIN

Christians
GET TO CELEBRATE
Passover
TOO!

Learning its Secrets, Power and Abundant Blessings

KENNETH S. ALBIN

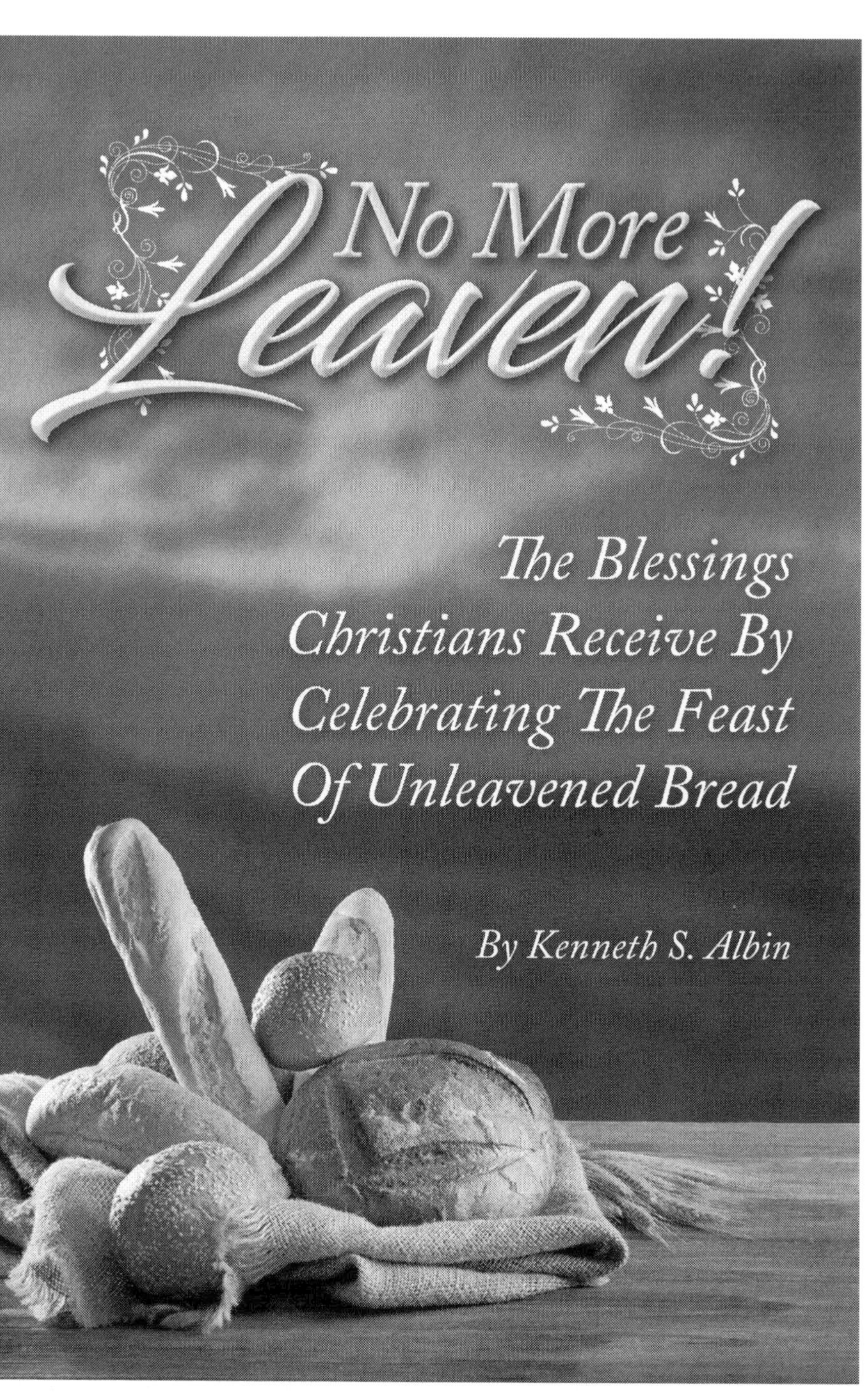
No More
Leaven!
The Blessings
Christians Receive By
Celebrating The Feast
Of Unleavened Bread
By Kenneth S. Albin

REVEALED

A Christian Understanding for Celebrating
the Biblical Holidays of Rosh Hashanah and Yom Kippur

BY KENNETH S. ALBIN

HANUKKAH *and PURIM*

ARE FOR CHRISTIANS TOO!

KENNETH S. ALBIN

HIT THE MARK

HOW CHRISTIANS CAN WALK IN THE MYSTERIES OF THE TORAH

AND RECEIVE ALL ITS BLESSINGS

HEALTH

ABUNDANT LIFE

PURPOSE-HAPPINESS-PEACE

KENNETH S. ALBIN

THE MYSTERY

OF THE CROWN

"WHY CHRIST HAD TO RECEIVE IT &
HOW ITS SECRETS CAN CHANGE YOUR WORLD."

FOREWORD BY TED SHUTTLESWORTH

HOW INTENTIONALLY GOING LOWER CAN TAKE YOU HIGHER

UPSIDE DOWN

FOREWORD BY
DR. MARK
CHIRONNA

KENNETH S. ALBIN

КАК, ОПУСКАЯСЬ ВНИЗ, ПОДНИМАТЬСЯ ВЫШЕ!
СНИЗУ
ВВЕРХ
ПРЕДИСЛОВИЕ
Д-РА МАРКА
ЧИРОННЫ
КЕННЕТ С. АЛБИН

KENNETH STEVEN ALBIN

YOU ARE BORN FOR THE **EXTRAORDINARY**

FOREWORD BY DR. SAMUEL CHAND

DISCOVER YOUR GREATER PURPOSE AND WALK IN THE BOOK WRITTEN OF YOUR LIFE

KENNETH S. ALBIN

It's a Celebration & Not Just an Option

How Christians can celebrate this Biblical Feast and the True Birthday of Messiah

Made in the USA
Middletown, DE
15 April 2022